TO HUSBANDS

THE part which a husband must play in life is not exactly an easy one. He has definite obligations and numerous restrictions. Often he will be puzzled as to why things have gone wrong.

This small volume of Do's and Don'ts should help to guide him away from errors and pitfalls, since it epitomises the correct conduct of husbands.

How to be a

Good
Husband

Bodleian Library
UNIVERSITY OF OXFORD

This edition first published in 2008 by the Bodleian Library
Broad Street, Oxford OX1 3BG
www.bodleianbookshop.co.uk
Reprinted 2008 (twice), 2009, 2010 (twice), 2011 (twice),
2012 (twice)

ISBN: 978 1 85124 376 1

This edition © Bodleian Library, University of Oxford, 2008
Originally published as *Do's and Don'ts for Husbands*, by
Universal Publications Ltd in 1936.
Images adapted from illustrations in Army and Navy
catalogues from 1933 and 1934 taken from the John Johnson
Collection in the Bodleian Library, University of Oxford;
Women's Clothes and Millinery 8 (24) and (25) respectively.

Cover design by Dot Little
Internal design by JCS Publishing Services Ltd,
www.jcs-publishing.co.uk
Printed and bound in China by C&C Offset Printing Co. Ltd.

British Library Catalogue in Publishing Data
A CIP record of this publication is available from the British
Library

CONTENTS

I

Don't lose sight of the fact that, once a man is married, the only sensible thing for him to do is to make the best of the circumstances. If his wife has faults, he should try to shut his eyes to them. It may be that he is not entirely perfect.

Don't allow yourself to grow indifferent to your wife. You once thought she was everything in the world and she is still the same person. A little encouragement from you will generally act like magic and draw you both together again.

Of course, you must not expect your wife to be perfect. There are no perfect wives and no perfect husbands. And even perfection would be a little tiring, if it did exist. So don't brood over the fact that your wife has her faults.

Don't act the lord and master to your wife. You may be both of these to her, but even if you are, no wife wants the fact rammed down her throat. Even if she wants you to be her lord and master, she would rather you called it co-partnership.

If you want your wife to be a real companion to you and take an interest in all you do, don't keep her in the dark about things. Tell her where you go, what you have seen and what you did. If she begins to feel that she must mind her own business, you will gradually drift apart.

Don't be the type of husband who has no time for his wife. If you work all day and dash off somewhere at night by yourself, she will eat her heart out and, when it is all consumed, you will be just the one to cry out about her departed love. Make some of her recreations yours and, then, you will be able to spend some of your leisure together.

No wife looks at everything from the same point of view as her husband does. She has her own point of view and the husband has his. So, if you know a thing is black, don't be surprised if your wife says it is white. At any rate, don't fly into a rage because she is so silly. Just agree to differ.

Don't tell your wife terminological inexactitudes, which are, in plain English, lies. A woman has a wonderful intuition for spotting even minor departures from the truth, and however much she has an aptitude for indulging in them herself, she scorns the male who utters them. Lying to her is a sign of weakness and weakness in a man she regards as a crime.

Don't let your wife get the impression that you feel superior because you earn the money. If this idea grows on her, she will regard you as a cad. After all, it is just as important in this world to know how to cook as to work at an office desk. And running a home is not all honey: it can be fairly puzzling at times.

Therefore, if your wife can cook and sew, take your hat off to her.

And while talking of money, tell your wife all about your finances and don't hide the figures from her. We once knew a man who would never tell his wife how much he earned and the silly fellow was always complaining that she never helped him to save. How could she help him when she was never allowed to know just where he stood?

Don't be a fault-finding husband. Of course, faults have to be pointed out at times, because after all no wife is absolutely perfect. A blind-eye is very useful on most occasions, but when you really must mention some defect, choose your time judiciously. If your wife has had a tiring day, leave the "curtain-lecture" for another time.

If you have a temper—and most of us have something of the sort—tell your wife when you feel irritable. If she is wise, she will do one of two things: she will either give you a wide berth or she will humour you. The first deprives you of the opportunity of venting your feelings and the second reveals to you what a gem of a wife you have. Above all, tell her when you are bad tempered and don't leave her to find it out.

If your wife becomes dowdy, don't blame her. She would not dare to wear "anything", if you were the kind of husband who had always made a point of telling her when she looked nice. In her mind, she argues that you never notice what she wears, so what does it matter?

Don't tell your wife that you love her dearly, and then, treat her as though she were dirt. She would much prefer you to say nothing and express your admiration by actions. Of course, most wives don't object to being told the fact, if all the actions go to support it. Even then, they don't want to hear about it too often.

Things have got to a pretty bad pitch if a wife's eyes do not sparkle, when her husband brings her home some unexpected trifle. So don't forget, a bunch of flowers, a box of sweets, a bottle of scent, or something quite personal, every now and again.

Don't be afraid of admitting the fact, when you are wrong. If you go to your wife and say to her: "I was in the wrong, yesterday evening, I'm sorry," she will look upon you as a strong man. And that means a lot to a woman.

Don't try to regulate your wife's friends. Give her the credit of being able to choose them sensibly—even though some of them belong to your own sex. If you put down your foot, it will only make her angry and then determined. And that is the sure road to open warfare.

Don't be a husband who treats his wife coarsely. Most women have a much greater regard for refinement than men have, and lapses in this direction are bound to give them an unpleasant shock.

Don't be a musty sort of fellow with nothing bright and fresh in your outlook. It must be a dreadful blow to a woman who pictures her husband as a knight in shining armour to have to realise that he is a dull sort of individual without aims and ambitions.

Work up an enthusiasm for something in which your wife can take an interest. That will help you both.

Relations are often the cause of a good deal of dissension and you must exercise all the wisdom of Solomon, and more, in approaching the "in-law" problems.

Don't, for instance, be like a bear with a sore head when your wife's mother arrives on the scene and, then, expect your wife to be all-smiles when it's your own mother's turn to visit you. Your mother may be a hundred times as nice as her mother, but will your wife be able to see it?

And when your mother-in-law departs, and your wife gives a sigh of relief, don't duplicate the expression of relief. Be absolutely passive for, while your wife may cast stones at her own people, she will thoroughly resent it if you take a hand at the game, also. It is a privilege of hers, not yours.

Then, there are your own people to think about. Your sisters, for instance, may be absolutely charming. If they are, let your wife find that out for herself. Don't tell her that they possess all the virtues and, certainly, don't ram the fact down her throat. If you do, she will grow to hate them and it will be largely your own fault.

Don't grumble because your wife insists on going over, with you, all the little trivialities of the past day. You may be tired and don't want to be bothered with what the butcher boy did or what the neighbour said. But look at it from the wife's point of view. If that is all she has to think about, it is high time you took her to the pictures or the theatre, and gave her something to fill her mind.

And, lastly, if you are wondering which is the better, a car in the garage or a kiddie in the cot, don't hesitate to choose the latter. The car may appeal to you no end; but, for a real purpose in life, the kiddie will beat it all hollow.

II

DON'T tell your wife the good story that Smith gave you if you wouldn't have told it her before you were married. By so doing you lower yourself in her eyes, and further show that your respect for her is not what it used to be. Don't fall into the error of thinking that because "it's only husband and wife" it doesn't matter.

Do not neglect to give credit occasionally where it is due. Think over your wife's job sometimes and ask yourself how you would like to do it.

Don't force your own opinion on your wife—even if you know that it's right—to the extent of being cruel. If she is certain there is a burglar downstairs get up and look round, and reassure her on the point—otherwise she may lie awake the greater part of the night in a state of terror.

Do refrain from treating your wife as a plaything, endeavouring to wrap her in cotton wool, or sheltering her from every wind that blows. After all she is your co-partner and as such you should allow her to shoulder a certain amount of responsibility.

Do take care not to make fun of your wife's little foibles in front of other people. She may join in the joke, and laugh at them herself, but you are asking for a bad ten minutes when your visitors have gone.

Do make a point of remembering all anniversaries. To forget your wife's birthday or the wedding anniversary is, in her eyes, a crime little short of treason and one which you will have the greatest trouble in expiating.

Do not neglect to give that kiss on leaving in the morning or on returning at night, and don't let it develop into a mere peck. Take care too that it doesn't become part of a mere routine but retains its warmth.

Do make a note of the fact that a little present unexpected is much more delightful to a wife than a big one long expected.

Don't allow your wife to have to repeat a request that is reasonable. To use the old army phrase, "Jump to it".

Do learn the lesson of bearing and forbearing quite early in your married life. Remember those lines of Cowper:

The kindest and the happiest pair
Will find occasion to forbear;
And something, every day they live,
To pity, and perhaps forgive.

Don't trouble your wife to do something which you can just as easily do for yourself. She is your co-partner not your servant.

Don't become thoughtless regarding your immediate circle and especially as regards your wife. Take to heart the words of Sir Humphrey

Davy: "Life is made up, not of great sacrifices or duties, but of little things, in which smiles and kindnesses and small obligations, given habitually, are what win and preserve the heart, and secure comfort."

Do at times recall the happy hours of your early love when you were only too happy to have the privilege of fetching and carrying. Still make it your duty and pleasure to open the door, carry the heavy parcel, place the chair at the table and generally give the right of way to your wife.

Don't reserve your best manners for special occasions and persons outside the family. Remember that your wife has always the first claim on them.

Don't forget that the only way to domestic happiness is the cultivation by both parties of absolute unselfishness.

Don't allow yourself to be angry at the same time as your wife or certainly the rift will be made worse. Further, don't shout at her unless the house is on fire.

Do take occasion at times to tell your wife that you still love her. Because she is a woman she likes to hear it and to be assured of it.

Do realise that a little persuasion will attain far better results than a lot of compulsion. A woman is like tar, only melt her and she will take any form in which you like to mould her.

Don't ever taunt your wife with a past mistake. Let the dead past bury its dead.

Don't forget that a man shows himself a true gentleman, and to his best advantage, when he takes a pleasure in waiting on his wife and carrying out gladly little services for her.

Do try, if in any way angry with each other, to follow out the old Scriptural injunction not to let the sun go down upon your wrath.

Don't talk at your wife either alone or in company, and don't be guilty of the meanness of making remarks at her expense. Don't forget that she belongs to you and to decry your own is the worst kind of foolishness.

Don't visit upon your wife the ill-humour caused by snubs or rebuffs that you have received during the day. This is only a cowardly form of retaliation. Remember that a woman possesses more delicate organisms and is made of finer clay than man. It is a well-known law of the animal kingdom that the male of the species always roars when he is irritated, but there is no need for you to bring yourself down to the level of the beast.

Do remember there can only be true happiness where there is self-denial. The ideal union is where each strives to yield to the reasonable wishes of the other.

III

Do take every care to make yourself a good conversationalist both at home and abroad. To be able to talk fluently and concisely has carried many men into good positions to which their abilities alone would never have entitled them.

Don't fall into the vulgar and common error of talking for the sake of talking. Try to achieve brevity in your conversation. Express your thoughts in as few words as possible, and if you want to carry conviction don't repeat yourself. In the case of most people their conversation would best begin where they mean to leave off.

Don't consider that conversation is something which you should monopolise. Give other people a chance. Some people's idea of conversation is a never-ending monologue.

Don't be so anxious to come in with something smart that you pay no attention to what is being said. The result will probably be that your comment, when uttered, will be quite irrelevant.

Do be careful not to criticise the imperfections of other people even if they are apparently strangers to the company you are in at the moment. You can never be certain in this world of who's who.

Don't boast of the success of your children or your relatives. It's only a form of boosting yourself.

Don't let your conversation be of the type that has been described as honey abroad and vinegar at home. Preserve your nicest sentiments for those who belong to you.

Do be careful to be kind in your talk of others. Follow the example of Joubert who wrote: "When my friends are blind of one eye I look at them in profile."

Don't break in when someone else is speaking. A good listener is always appreciated. Learn to take your share of listening as well as talking.

Don't be a person with a grievance if you wish to be popular. The world hasn't much time for the person who harps on one string.

Don't let all your remarks savour of criticism. A little of this sort of thing is perhaps bracing but too much of it will cause depression.

Don't forget that if you have to tell a home truth it should only be necessary to tell it once and not to re-tell it. Further, if it is not a pleasant one try to tell it with tact and sympathy. Don't, unless in the very exceptional case, rub it in.

Do remember that loud argument is one of the most common signs of faulty education and ill-breeding.

Don't pride yourself on the fact that you always speak as you feel. It is more than probable that you do nothing of the kind, and if you do it won't be long before you upset someone. An ounce of tact will usually carry you much farther than a ton of such speaking.

Do endeavour to keep your temper even when your views are opposed by those with whom you are conversing. You may of course be right—but so may they.

Don't allow yourself when engaged in conversation to be self-conscious or shy. If you fix your mind on what you are going to say your nervousness will disappear.

Do be careful how you discuss mutual friends with someone else. Words often become strangely twisted in the course of transit and sometimes bear no resemblance to their original signification.

Don't discuss personal affairs in general conversation and try to steer clear of the personal affairs of other people. Matters that may be of great interest to you are not necessarily so to others.

Don't attempt to help out the man who is somewhat slow of expression by finishing his sentences for him. It implies that in this matter you consider yourself very much his superior.

Don't allow yourself to become careless in your conversation and, as far as possible, don't use the cant expressions of the moment. Try to avoid describing a thing as "awfully nice" or "putrid".

IV

PERSONAL HABITS

DON'T squeeze the tube of tooth paste from the top instead of from the bottom. This is one of the small things of life that always irritates a careful wife.

Do remember to shake out your pipe and put down your book a little earlier than usual if your wife has had a troublesome day with baby and is likely to have to get up and attend to him once or twice during the night.

Do, if you wish for happiness, refrain from adopting the attitude of "that's my way and so you must put up with it". Your wife may allow you to drop cigarette ash all over the house, or leave everything just where you have finished

29

with it, but it won't make her any better pleased with you.

Don't confine your acts of courtesy to your wife's pretty girl friends. Be as ready to see Miss Prudence Dowdy, who is very much of a bore, back to her home as you would the charming Miss Dolly Dimple.

Don't think that your wife has placed waste-paper baskets in the rooms as ornaments. They are put there for you to use. Don't, however, utilise them for spent matches unless you are very well insured.

Don't—if you have no business that takes you abroad—be always about the house. Have a fixed period during which you go out or go away into your den. Remember that even if you have no calls on your time your wife has her daily round of duties to get through and, pleasurable as your company may be, there is always the possibility of having too much of a good thing. It is surprising how many wives who love their husbands look forward with dread to the day of their retirement from business.

Do cultivate the habit of believing in yourself if you wish others to believe in you. Let your outlook on life be hopeful, cheery and optimistic.

Don't get into the habit of storing up a lot of useless old stuff and then grumble for a week if your wife disposes of some of it. Every woman likes her house to be a home not a marine store depot. Have an occasional overhaul of your belongings and clear out what is useless. You won't require three old hats and four old suits for garden wear.

Don't be one of those persons who try to run their own life and that of everyone around them according to programme. They usually only succeed in making everyone miserable. Bring a little give and take into life.

Do remember that if you are going to get the best out of life you must overlook a great many things. Your standard is not that of everyone, nor will they see with your eyes. Try sometimes to look at matters from the point of view of the other person.

Do try not to waste time and energy on the non-essentials of life but to concentrate on the essentials. Don't be one of those persons who flies into a passion and upsets the whole house because someone has taken a book from one shelf of the bookcase and put it back on another. The energy you have spent in railing against this little slip would probably be sufficient to do that pressing job in the garden that you have neglected so long.

Do be careful in your choice of friends. Instinctively, we absorb from them their qualities, and if these are not good there will inevitably be a decline in our character.

Do cultivate the habit of coming down to breakfast with a smile. Remember that, as the head of the house, it is your duty to see that everyone starts the day in an atmosphere of happiness.

Don't refrain from singing in your bath if you feel like it. Your wife will welcome it since it's a sign that the barometer is at "set fair".

Do try not only to give out sunshine to others but to imbibe it. Cultivate by every means in your power the sunny side of your nature. Learn to join in the joy of others and to make it your own. Don't reply simply "Yes" when your little daughter asks if you don't think her new doll is lovely. Spread yourself a little in your reply. Share her enthusiasm and you will double her joy.

Do be not only courteous but properly courteous. If you don't want to be mistaken for a groom don't raise your hat by touching the brim. Raise it clear of the head for a moment.

Don't expect to be numbered among the good mannered if you use a nail file, comb or toothpick otherwise than in a dressing-room.

Don't omit, if seated, to rise when introduced either to a lady or a gentleman. Life is not so short that it does not provide time enough for courtesy.

Don't forget that courtesy is always in fashion and always good form. The small courtesies sweeten life, the greater ennoble it.

Do remember that kindness is a passport which will take you anywhere in the world. It is the golden chain by which society is bound together.

Do try to leave your room as neat as you can. If you don't you can't grumble if your things are not put back in the place where you expect to find them. You may be untidy in your office—though this is not advisable—but home is a different matter.

Don't be so anxious to get on in the world that you've no time for anything else. Success will probably turn to ashes, if by the time you find you have attained your desire you realise that you are almost a stranger to your wife and children. To work hard for your wife and family is quite laudable, but in doing so preserve a well-balanced mind and give them their fair share of your time and your attention.

Don't be one of those persons who blame but never praise. If your wife makes some little dish of which you are very fond, don't omit to show your appreciation. If she looks

34

particularly nice on some occasion don't hesitate to tell her so. A little attention to such things makes the wheels of life run much more smoothly.

V

DRESS AND CLOTHING

DON'T make the common mistake of thinking that indifference to dress denotes either individuality or humility. In most cases it is simply a form of silly pride. Moreover don't forget that neglect of it is not much of a compliment to either your wife or family. Bear in mind the old couplet:

Virtue may flourish in an old cravat
But men and Nature scorn the shocking
  hat.

Do be careful in your general turn-out. To be badly groomed or improperly dressed carries with it a certain sense of inferiority and therefore loss of power. You can never hope to succeed to the full where there is such loss of energy and of self-confidence.

Don't allow yourself to become careless in the matter of dress in the home, nor permit your wife to be so. To sit down to dinner in the hot weather in your shirt-sleeves may be very comfortable, but no nice woman looks with equanimity on any action that her husband would hesitate to do in the presence of other women.

Don't fall into the error of thinking that the possession of much jewellery marks you as a person of consequence. The wearing of this by men has now gone out of fashion, and where precious stones are worn they should be of the smallest. At the most, one good ring is the limit allowed by good taste.

Don't endeavour to persuade your wife to refuse invitations because the acceptance will mean that you have to put on your dress-clothes. This is pure selfishness on your part, so for once put your own inclinations on one side and give her a chance of wearing her pretty frocks.

Do be careful not to wear a made-up tie with evening wear or coloured socks with evening shoes. The latter should be plain black silk.

Don't forget that if you are in doubt as regards the wearing of tails or a dinner-jacket, the former is always in better taste, except in the case of an informal dinner.

Do be careful when selecting a striped tie not to purchase the colours of some famous school or club. It is somewhat awkward to be taken for a Guards officer when the nearest claim you can make to belonging to the Services is that you were once a Boy Scout.

Don't neglect your wife's advice on matters pertaining to your own dress. As a rule a woman knows better than a man what suits him, and in any case she knows what she prefers.

Don't grumble when your wife raises the question of a new hat and go on to point out that your present one has lasted you two years. The wearing by a woman of a hat and other things, even only six months behind the fashion, announces to all her friends that she is the unfortunate possessor of a stingy husband.

Do make every endeavour that your dress shall be neat, quiet and suitable for the occasion. These are the three essential qualities for a well-dressed man.

Don't forget also that a man is well dressed when you don't know what he is wearing. To dress in a conspicuous manner usually means that the person guilty of it has run off the rails of good taste.

Don't omit to make a note of the fact that soft shirts should never be worn with full dress.

Don't wear a white waistcoat with a dinner-jacket. The experiment has been tried, but it soon died a natural death.

Do take care that you never wear a blazer with anything but white flannels, even if the crest on it is gorgeous enough to stagger humanity.

Do remember that the use of a comb in public is always offensive and against the canons of good taste.

Do, when going out with your wife, dress with the same care that you used to do before you were married. Even if a woman has been married twenty years, she still takes a pride in seeing her man well turned out.

Don't turn up to tea in your old garden coat when your wife has some particular friends coming. It won't take a minute or two to run upstairs and change it and your wife will think a lot more of you for this deference to her wishes. Remember that it is often the little sacrifices that appeal to women more than the bigger ones.

Don't stick to a style of dress that your wife doesn't like. You may think you look very "nutty" in your somewhat loud plus fours, but if she says they don't suit you she is probably right.

41

Don't expect your wife to make a dress last as long as your mother does. The dear old lady has probably now reached the age when she only wishes to be clothed, whereas your wife is still young enough to be dressed.

Do try not to be conservative in the matter of your wife's dresses. Because you liked the blue dress that she wore when you first met her don't suggest that she should always adopt that colour. Dress is about the one thing in which a woman likes to be adventurous, so let her have her way even if you don't agree with the result.

Don't forget that little adjuncts to dress are always acceptable to a woman. You may not be able to afford a fur coat but an occasional pair of gloves is always a delight.

Don't be careless and go to the office in that grease-spotted coat. If noticed there, it won't be put down to your credit. A little time and petrol is all that is required.

VI

DON'T think that because you earn the money you are entitled to spend the bulk of it on yourself. Remember that you are partners in a joint concern and that your wife has as much right to her proper share as you have to yours. Don't let the onetime promise "with all my worldly goods I thee endow" be entirely forgotten.

Do try, as far as lies in your power, to give your wife a set sum for house-keeping and another for her own personal use. It is very lowering to her dignity to have to ask you for money every time she wants to buy a pair of

43

gloves or make a small present to anyone. Give her as good an allowance as you can for dress and pocket money and impress upon her the necessity of keeping within it.

Don't be so absorbed in making a living that you have no time to make a life.

Do take care not to be led into expenses that you cannot afford in order to keep up appearances. The attempt to do this is only too often accompanied by vulgarity and disastrous consequences.

Don't be led into the error of buying things simply because they are cheap. If you don't really want them they are dear at any price.

Don't grudge spending money on labour-saving devices. It should be your endeavour to do anything you can to lighten your wife's daily round.

Do avoid the somewhat common practice of having a joint banking account on which you can both draw. Let your wife have a separate account and you will then both know just how you stand.

Don't let economising be something which the wife alone has to do. See what you can do as regards cutting down your own personal expenses. Watch your expenditure on tobacco, drinks and amusements.

Don't cut down the household allowance and then grumble because things are not as they were. You can't eat your cake and have it, and your wife can't increase the value of a pound to thirty shillings.

Don't let all your energies be spent upon mere money making. There are other things that matter such as beauty and love and it should be your endeavour to put these into your life.

Do try as far as possible to avoid letting accounts run. It's probably not so easy to pay in a month's time as it is to-day. Endeavour to settle on a weekly basis and see that your wife does the same.

Don't forget that the quality that will do you most harm financially is pride. Probably the largest proportion of bankruptcies come from those who have gone beyond their means in pretending that they are what they really are not.

Don't do all the ordering because you think that your wife is wanting in the money sense. This lowers both her dignity and her position. Take a little trouble to teach her, and let her realise that she must cut her coat according to her cloth.

Do take care not to hand out the household allowance as if you were parting with money for which you get little value. If you are not satisfied, go through the bills with your wife and thrash the matter out thoroughly.

Don't run your finances on a haphazard principle. Take your weekly income and split it up into rent and rates, household expenditure, wife's allowance, savings and extras, and then stick to such allotments. If you adhere rigidly to this you will never have those unexpected bills that you cannot meet.

Don't forget that life is full of the unexpected. Make provision for such things as doctor's bills, replacements and breakages. (See extras in preceding paragraph.)

Do make a start, directly you get married, to insure your life. Whatever happens, your wife will then have something to fall back upon.

VII

HEALTH

Do remember that in the preservation of health there is no agent so powerful as work. "Work", writes Dean Farmer, "is the best birthright that man still retains. It is the strongest of moral tonics, the most vigorous of mental medicines."

Don't worry yourself into a low condition by mourning over past failures. Turn your back on the shadows and face the light. If there is a fancied skeleton in the cupboard inter it decently and then flood the place with sunshine.

Do steer clear of any form of recreation which results in your snapping everyone's

head off at the breakfast-table and which sends you to your work unrefreshed, languid and in the worst of tempers.

Do realise that if you really are out of sorts there is no necessity to take it out of the family. Your wife has probably enough to do nursing you without having to put up with your ill-temper as well.

Don't allow yourself as the years go on to give way and grow slack. Try to preserve that firm step and straight back as long as you possibly can. In the first place it's a great adjunct to health, and in the second you don't want to lose the pride which your wife took in these matters.

Do suppress that tendency to fidget, not so much for the sake of your own health as for that of your wife's. We all know the type of man (and woman) who is never quiet for a moment, but whose hands or feet are constantly in motion. Such a condition is certainly not good for your own nerves and is doubly worse for those around you.

Don't sit up late, rise late, and then have to run to the office after half a breakfast. No machinery works well if subjected to intermittent strain and stress.

Don't go on when Nature tells you plainly that it's time to call a halt. The constant headache, the general feeling of lassitude, the need for a stimulant of some kind and the irritability with every one are Nature's danger signals and, if disregarded, calamity will inevitably follow.

Don't think that you can outrage Nature and then put matters right with a few doses of some patent medicine. Her demands are few in number, moderation in eating and drinking and sufficient outdoor exercise and sufficient rest, but if you don't give her these you can certainly look out for trouble.

Do take care not to be one of those persons who are always worrying over their health. If you feel really ill go and see the doctor, but don't refuse to do so and then continue to worry your wife by vague surmises as to what is the matter with you. It's remarkable how many ailments disappear if you engross yourself in something that deeply interests you.

Do guard yourself against becoming a faddist. Everyone realises the benefit of cold baths for those who can stand them, but to take it when you are far from being well, because it is your custom to take a daily one, is the action of a lunatic. Similarly if you are somewhat of a fresh air fiend don't insist on bringing the temperature of the house down to freezing point. Although you can stand it other people perhaps can't, and they have a right to be considered also.

Don't forget that as regards both yourself and your family, prevention is better than cure. Twenty-four hours delay in calling in a doctor is often attended by very serious consequences.

Don't be so foolish as to refuse to wear glasses because you think you look a fright in them, and don't temporise by wearing a monocle when what you require is spectacles.

Don't be impatient as regards the illnesses of those around you. Because you have perfect health there is no reason why you need be unsympathetic.

Do remember that to do certain things at fifty means a much greater strain than to do them at forty. Although you may appear to be in the best of health take stock of yourself occasionally and in the course of it ask yourself if all your habits and pursuits are such as are suitable to your years. If not, have a re-adjustment and drop any that may be injurious.

VIII

CHILDREN

DON'T let the children look upon you as a grave and solemn person. Unbend sometimes and have a good romp with them. You may find your joints a little stiff afterwards but you will be surprised to find how light it makes your heart.

Don't omit to show the children a good example. Remember they always copy their elders. To make them considerate, thoughtful and courteous let them see you displaying these qualities on all occasions.

Do take the utmost care always to honour your wife in the presence of the children. If they hear you constantly snapping her up or

contradicting her the inevitable result will be that before long they will lose their respect for her and you.

Don't allow one child to interrupt another who is reading or studying. To ensure peace and comfort in a family each one must realise that consideration for others is an absolute essential.

Don't find fault unless it is quite certain that a fault has been committed and then speak reprovingly but, at the same time, lovingly. Never punish on mere suspicion, but if guilt is not proved give the benefit of the doubt. Children have a very keen sense of justice and the memory of an unmerited punishment will rankle for years. It was undoubtedly a person with no knowledge of the child mind who first suggested that to give a boy an unearned punishment didn't matter as he was bound to earn it before long.

Do be careful never to countermand any order which your wife has already given to the children. To do so is only to lower her in their eyes and to give them the impression that they can play off one of you against the other.

Don't be impatient when any of the children are fretful or sick. Your wife has quite enough to put up with without your adding to her troubles and the probability is that when you have a headache you are no saint yourself.

Don't allow one member of the family to interrupt another when telling a tale or narrating some experience. Elder children are sometimes given to repressing the younger ones in this respect and this should be stopped at once.

Do encourage your children to take their part in the table conversation. Never act on that idiotic old saying that children should be seen and not heard. At the same time do not let them over-ride the conversation and repress at once any tendency to shout at one another.

Don't forget that the family table is the last place in the world where there should be any unpleasant remarks made. Nothing is worse for digestion than trouble or worry. Let your dinner table be the happy gathering point for the family. See to it that there is no vulgar chipping or decrying of the talents of one member of the family by the others.

Don't pay heavy school fees and at the same time neglect the home discipline. The one is just as important as the other. Family life has been well described as God's own method of training the young.

Do insist that at all times the boys pay proper respect to their mother and sisters. Don't permit too much teasing of the latter or let the boys think that women run secondary in the scheme of things. See that they always spring to open the door for their mother. The boy who is brought up to pay proper respect to women will find himself welcome and at ease in any good class of society.

Don't forget in all your dealings with the children that kind words are the music of the world.

Don't make a decision and then alter it because one of the children whines or coaxes. Once they realise that this method may be successful they will protest in some form or other at everything which they don't like. Decide on the course you mean to take and then stick to it.

Don't allow children to be importunate in their demands. If they are, and you give way, they will expect more and more.

Do take the utmost care that each member of the family respects the others' privacy. Neglect of this generally means loss of temper and loss of self-respect. Let each person's room, drawer, or even play-box, be inviolate and not to be touched by others without permission.

Do endeavour to be as pleasant at your own table as you would be if you were a guest at that of someone else. Surely you should pay as much respect to your own as you would to others. Besides, don't forget that you largely set the standard for the household.

Don't be a prohibitive father. The parent who tells the children ten times what they must not do for only once what they may do should not be surprised if they come to look upon him as somewhat of a spoilsport, if not an ogre.

Do as far as possible try to help, and not hinder, natural influences. The boy with a natural aptitude for making things may at times cause a good deal of muddle in the house, but if you repress him entirely you may be suppressing the genius of a born engineer.

Don't punish the children when you are busy, tired, hungry or vexed. Wait until you are in a frame of mind when you can act judicially.

Don't send the children to such an expensive school that you can't afford to let them indulge in the same sports, etc., as their schoolfellows. Children are often terrible snobs and will rub in the fact that one of them cannot do the same as the others. This may probably give rise to an inferiority complex that will last through life. Send them to a school where they can join with others on an equal footing.

Don't spend all your money on the training of the boys and leave the girls with an inferior education. They have just as much right to their fair share and in these days it is just as necessary.

Don't get the idea that what was good enough for you in your youth should be good enough for your children. Times have moved since then. On the other hand don't start them where you left off. A little hard struggle at the beginning tends to form character.

IX

RECREATIONS

DON'T laugh when you find going shopping with your wife placed under this heading. It is her recreation, and she will think all the more of you if occasionally you put your own inclinations on one side and join forces with her in something in which she is interested.

Do take care that the car doesn't become the leading feature in your life. See that the possession of it doesn't affect adversely the things in which you formerly took pride such as your house and garden, or, even more important, that it curtails expenditure in things which are much more necessary.

Don't insist upon your wife being always a passenger. Teach her to drive. A long journey is much more enjoyable to both if you can share the labour.

Do endeavour as far as possible to take up the same recreations. This will give you a joint interest and make you the greater pals.

Don't laugh at your wife's recreations, although they may seem to you absurd. While you are wondering what pleasure she sees in spending two or three hours at a sewing meeting she, on her part, cannot conceive how you can waste your time at that Masonic meeting or public dinner. Don't forget the old adage, "*chacun à son goût*".

Don't, when once you are married, continue a recreation that is highly dangerous. The wife of a man who finds his hobby in motor racing or mountain climbing must often have some very anxious moments.

Do be careful as you grow older not to drop all athletic pursuits unless you want to see your toes gradually disappearing from view.

Most women like their husbands to keep slim and fit even with advancing years. Strive to keep your youthful vigour as long as you can.

Do endeavour that at least one of your hobbies is of the description that can be carried out within the home, but, on the other hand, don't let it engross every minute of your time. Take care also that it is not of the type that demands that you shall not be in any way interrupted and imposes silence on the rest of the household.

Don't take up a hobby which entails your getting the pleasure and other people the work pertaining to it. There are some men who claim that their hobby is gardening, but while they leave their wives to do the actual digging their part is restricted to sitting in an armchair and turning it over in their mind.

Don't, unless for some very good reason, put a veto on any recreation your wife may wish to take up. After all she must have pretty good judgment since she elected to marry you. You wouldn't be at all pleased if she wanted to put her foot on some recreation of yours which in your opinion was particularly desirable.

Do refrain from smiling in a superior manner if your wife wishes to attend lectures or classes. Of course you don't require any further knowledge, but let her alone if she thinks she does. At any rate it will give her an interest and she will be a better companion than the wife who only gets her ideas from feminine tea-party chatter.

Don't forget that a sensible hobby tends to longevity. There may come a time when you have perforce to give up your daily work or business and if you have no hobby to fill up your time you'll soon fall into the ranks of the arm-chair and slipper brigade.

Do, in choosing a hobby, select one which possesses the double merit of being out of doors and one in which your wife can join. This will give you health and community of interest.

Don't attempt to choose your wife's books for her if she is fond of reading. You may think that the reading of light literature is a waste of time, but to her it is a much needed relief from the daily round. Remember you are her husband and not her schoolmaster.

Don't, if your wife is fond of it, omit to learn to dance. If you are unable to join with her in this recreation half the pleasure will be lost to her. Further, in order not to drag you to something in which you cannot participate she will often feel compelled to stay at home when she would love to be dancing. Don't take the type of holiday that gives your wife just the same duties that she has at home. You may like a camping holiday but first ask yourself if this is going to be a restful one for her and if it is going to give her a respite from the preparation of meals.

Do occasionally put your own inclinations on one side and go out with your wife in the evening to call on friends. Remember that you are mixing with people all day, but that she is more or less shut up in the house and gets little chance of mixing with others.

Don't spend every evening at the club and return home hoping to find your wife where Cain found his, that is, in the land of Nod. The probability is that she won't be able to go to sleep until you are safely at home.

Don't expect your wife to find all her relaxation in needlework or similar pursuits. She probably has ideas of her own and it is your duty, and should be your pleasure, to fall in with these as far as possible.

Don't take a furnished house for a holiday and at the same time send the maid away for hers. This may be a good arrangement so far as you are concerned, but its result will be that your wife will have a poor time.

Don't let your annual holiday be of the kind that leaves you more tired than when you started. Attempting to see the maximum in the minimum of time is more than foolish. Also, if cruising, don't cut your sleeping time down to the minimum by staying up late every night. Early to bed and early to rise is just as good a rule for the holiday as for the everyday life.

Don't buy a motor cycle and side-car without first consulting your wife. You may think it splendid to be able to cover so much more ground than you did on the two cycles, but you may find that she is nervous of your suggested means of locomotion. Further, perhaps she is quite content with the more limited range of the push-cycle and prefers the quiet companionable ride to the swift and less conversational rush through the countryside.

Don't let your wife's cycle become, after marriage, only a means of making a hurried run round the shops while you use yours to go off for long rides with your best chum. Take her with you, and even if it reduces your mileage the pleasure of her company will more than compensate.

X

DON'T forget when going to stay with friends to notify the hour of your arrival and whether coming by car or train. In the latter case they will require to know in order to make arrangements to meet you. Further, once you have announced the hour of your departure stick to it. You may be pressed to go at a later hour, but if you do agree there is the possibility that you may throw out the daily routine.

Don't commit the unpardonable sin of introducing your wife with "Meet the wife."

Do take particular care not to be late when invited to a card party. Remember that until you arrive the tables cannot be made up and

that consequently your late arrival is a slight to everyone present.

Don't omit when attending any functions, such as an at home or tea party, to assist the hostess as far as possible by attending on the ladies present.

Do refrain when playing cards from commenting on anyone's playing to another person. Post-mortems are never pleasant and it's a good rule to let the dead past bury its dead.

Don't when playing cards look scornful if the others have an objection to playing for high stakes or for playing for money at all. They have as much right as you to be considered.

Don't when going for a week-end be so careless in your packing that you find it necessary to borrow from your host. Make for the nearest shop or do without.

Do make every endeavour when staying at a boarding-house to fall in with the general temperament. Don't start to make whoopee among a community of elderly people or suggest cards on a Sunday in a house that is strictly Sabbatarian. Try and fit in with your environment.

Don't also discuss the shortcomings of the house with other guests. If you have a complaint to make let it be to the management, and if it is not sufficiently important for that then be silent.

Don't omit to allow your wife or any lady to precede you into a car or taxi, but take care to get out first in order to assist her to alight.

Don't forget also to allow your wife or any lady accompanying you to precede you in getting out of a lift.

Do remember in whatever company you may find yourself not to be stand-offish, critical, cynical or offensive. Don't associate yourself too closely with any particular clique, whether it is in a boarding-house, tennis club or dance hall.

Don't forget when motoring to acknowledge all signals given by other motorists and also make your own clear and distinct.

Do be considerate and, if your wife is nervous in a car, drive slowly. Don't laugh at her and then go full speed ahead in the idea that you will break her of this trait. By so acting you will only increase her nervousness and you certainly won't increase her love for you.

Don't be the owner of a noisy horn and don't sound it too much. The donkey who brays the loudest is not always the most useful animal.

Don't drive in such a manner as to raise clouds of dust, and don't drive so near the kerb on a wet day as to splash pedestrians. Although they may not possess a car they are still entitled to some consideration.

Don't make the mistake when invited to a birthday or christening party of taking your present with you. This should always be sent in advance.

Don't forget after you have stayed with friends to send the bread and butter letter as soon as possible after your return home. Endeavour also to make it something better than a mere thank you, and where your friends have made an extra effort to give you a good time take a little trouble to tell them how much you have appreciated it.

Do strive to get a character for punctuality in all your social engagements. Make it your endeavour to be always present five minutes before the hour fixed.

Don't omit when any lady leaves or enters the room to stand up and to remain so until the door is closed or she has sat down.

Do remember if you form the sudden idea of spending Whitsuntide or Easter at the seaside to give your wife sufficient warning. It's all very well to give her a nice surprise the day before but she won't thank you for so doing. You may think that it should only take a minute or two to pack a bag but there are one hundred and one arrangements about the house to be made which cannot be done at a moment's notice. Moreover there is always the momentous matter of dress to be decided.

Don't rush your wife off to some holiday resort at a time when it is likely to be crowded without making some arrangement beforehand for your accommodation. Long before you have walked round and found a home she will be worn out and all her pleasure gone, added to which the accommodation you will obtain in these circumstances will probably be of an inferior description.

Don't take your wife to a dance and then leave her to herself for the greater part of the evening while you spend a good time in the card room or the bar. If you do this you can hardly wonder if she complains that she wishes she had never come. Don't forget that your first duty is to see that she has a good time, and further that the world is quick to notice where a wife is neglected.

XI

ENTERTAINING

DON'T criticise the food at your own table when you are entertaining and especially refrain from doing it before the servants. To do so will only have the effect of making your wife unhappy, rendering your guests uncomfortable, and probably, repeated with additions, cause a small riot in the kitchen. Wait till your guests have departed and then consult as to the measures to be taken for improvement in the future.

Don't "tell off" a servant in the presence of your guests. It will make the latter feel uncomfortable and may result in the maid following the now common custom of "downing tools". In any case her service for the rest of the day will probably be marked by a surly or a tearful demeanour.

Do make a point of welcoming your wife's friends just as heartily as if they were your own. You may not like Mrs. B., but while she is under your roof it is the height of bad manners to even let her have a suspicion of the fact.

Don't forget that if your wife is entertaining lady guests it is your duty to escort them to the front door.

Do endeavour when introducing two guests to each other to bring up some subject in which they will both be interested. It is hardly sufficient to introduce them, remark on the weather, and then leave them to find a subject for themselves.

Don't entertain your visitors with a full and detailed account of your recent illness, giving them a graphic account of every pain you suffered. They have come to your house to be entertained, not to listen to an organ recital.

Don't attempt to give champagne suppers on a soda-water income. Your true friends won't appreciate your efforts as they will feel they are putting you to expense that you can ill afford, while your false friends will only put it down as "swank".

Do take care that your guests will not clash. Don't invite the elderly, stodgy and pompous, even if it is good for your business, at the same time as the young and frivolous. Much better divide it into two separate functions.

Don't chat on the door step with one departing guest, leaving the others to look after themselves.

Don't unduly press your guests to partake of everything on the table. This onetime custom now only exists among semi-civilised peoples. Don't also, in a spirit of false humility, decry what you have provided and suggest that it is not all that it should be. Do the best that you can reasonably afford and leave it at that.

Don't growl every time your wife proposes to ask a few friends in for the evening. You may think it a bit of a nuisance but you will spoil her pleasure if you let her see that you think so.

Do be careful not to make the mistake of telling your wife that you will be only too delighted if she will go to the pictures, theatre, etc., but that you don't care for that sort of thing and will stop at home and keep house. Prior to your marriage you would only have been too happy to have gone anywhere with her, and your refusal now cannot fail to hurt her. For once put your own wishes on one side and accompany her.

XII

THEATRES, DINNERS, AND RESTAURANTS

Do try to make a practice when taking your wife to the theatre of booking your seats in advance. This will often prevent you having to pay more than you intended and will obviate your wife having to wait while you stand in a queue.

Don't forget that you precede a lady to a theatre seat, but on reaching the row in which it is situated you stand on one side and allow her to go first.

Do bear in mind that most ladies like to get to their theatre seats at least five minutes before the curtain goes up in order that they can look around and see who is present and what they wear.

Don't forget that box of chocolates, and if she prefers a particular kind, which is probably not on sale in the theatre, take care to get them beforehand.

Don't leave your wife alone during the interval in order to go and get a drink. For once go without. Of course if she presses you to go that is a different matter, but satisfy yourself that her pressure is genuine. You will find that she appreciates your sacrifice.

Don't consider that you have done all that is necessary when you take your wife out to dinner or to a theatre. Pay her the further compliment of getting into dress clothes for the occasion. Such a compliment is one which will condone many of your other sins of omission.

Do be careful not to be too long in depositing your hat, etc., in the cloak-room if your wife is waiting for you. It is embarrassing for any lady to have to wait long in any such public place as the entrance hall of an hotel or theatre.

Don't forget that if following a waiter to a table a lady should precede her husband. If on the other hand they have to seek a table he should lead the way.

Don't omit, when taking your wife out to dinner at a restaurant, to mark the occasion by suggesting a bottle of wine. Remember that ladies usually prefer a sweet wine to a dry and that as regards liqueurs Crême de Menthe is always a favourite.

XIII

GENERAL

DON'T be proud of the fact that you can't carve and that you always leave it to your wife. It is the duty of the head of the house to undertake this task and by handing it over you confess that you play only the second fiddle.

Don't forget that marriage, like government, must be a series of compromises.

Do make every effort to show kindness whenever possible. Remember that Wordsworth wrote:

That best portion of a good man's life,
His little nameless, unremembered acts
   of kindness and of love.

Don't leave humour entirely out of your life. Remember that it is the lubricant which oils the machinery of life and makes it run smoothly.

Don't forget that you cannot make your presence felt so long as you are not master of yourself.

Do take care not to get into the habit of sighing over what might have been. Put it out of your mind and make the best of what is. Moreover it may possibly be that what might have been is not half such a rosy picture as your imagination paints it. What about adopting as your motto "The best is yet to be"?

Don't forget that the home is the one place where a man shows whether or not he is truly courteous. He may be a delightful companion abroad, his manners to the women he meets in society may be perfect, but if he is not considerate towards his own womenfolk his good form is only a veneer.

Do remember that if you aspire to the good old name of gentleman your conduct at all times must be marked by consideration for others. This is shown best not in the big things of life but in the little ones.

Do endeavour to take the rough things of life by the smooth handle.

Do try to cultivate the habit of enjoying things and finding pleasure in the small affairs of life. To be able always to look on the sunny side of life is worth far more than a fortune.

Don't look on life through smoked glasses. Bear in mind the following little verse:

Life's a mirror; if we smile,
Smiles come back to greet us;
If we're frowning all the while
Frowns forever meet us.

Don't cultivate the idea that your daily work is dreary and monotonous. Learn to find happiness in the doing of it and it will seem tenfold lighter. Do realise that all work is ennobling if we put our best into it.

Don't forget that the world has you always more or less under inspection. In this connection remember the words of Goethe: "Behaviour is a mirror in which everyone shows his image."

Don't grumble if marriage makes you neglect many of the things that you used to do when you were single. It is better to neglect the whole world than your wife. Moreover if you have chosen wisely you are much the gainer since a good wife has aptly been described as a gift bestowed upon man to reconcile him to the loss of Paradise.

Do take care that you don't make your wife pay too high a price for any success you may achieve. When this does arrive the rewards are in no sense equal since the husband gets the glory and the wife only the reflected glory.

Don't forget that two of the essentials to a happy married life are mutual affection and esteem. These cannot however exist for long unless there is mutual respect and consideration at all times and under all conditions.

Don't ever use that absurd phrase: "It's everyone for himself in this world." Remember that if this theory were generally practised we should still be in that now far-off age when men took what they wanted by the simple process of clubbing the other fellow on the head. If we accept the privileges of an organised society we must be prepared to do our share of giving to the common weal.

Do realise that if you are to get the full value out of life you must live it with all your faculties all the time. Until you come to the time when your physical faculties begin to fail you should so live your life that every day is just a little too short for what you purpose to do in it. There is a world of truth in the old saying that it's better to wear out than to rust out.